This is a coloring book,
which contains land, air and
water vehicles. also heavy
machinery

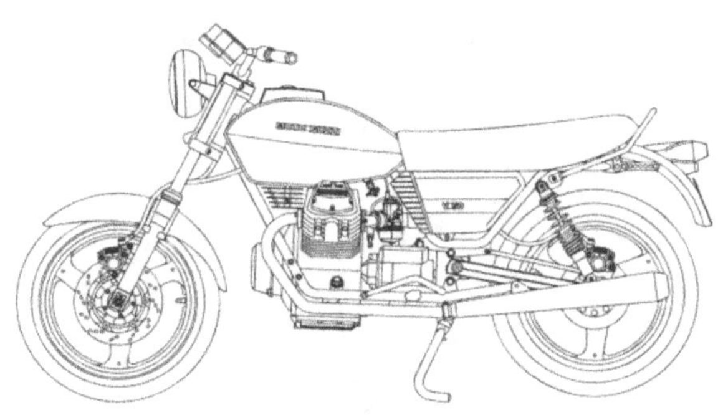

PLANE - AVION

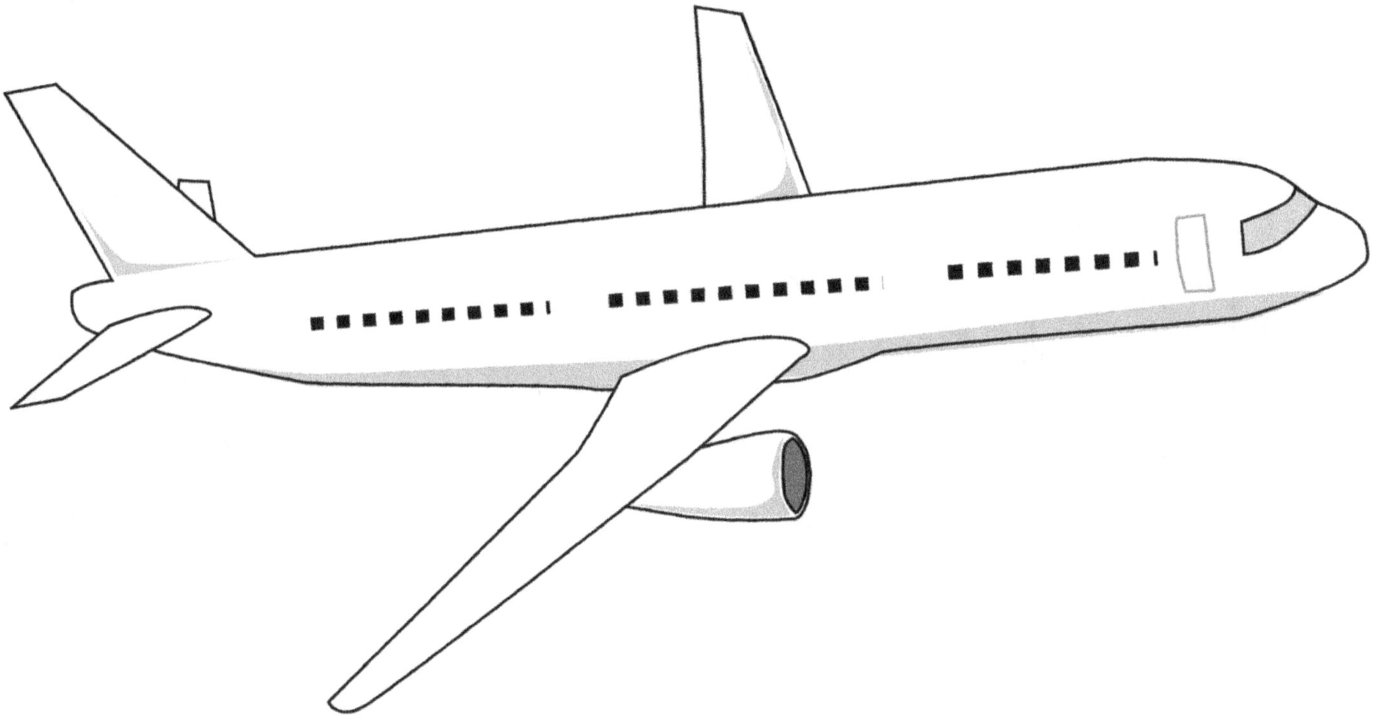

SHIP – BARCO

FIRE TRUCK – CAMION DE BOMBEROS

AMBULANCE – AMBULANCIA

CAMPER – FURGONETA

BUS – AUTOBUS

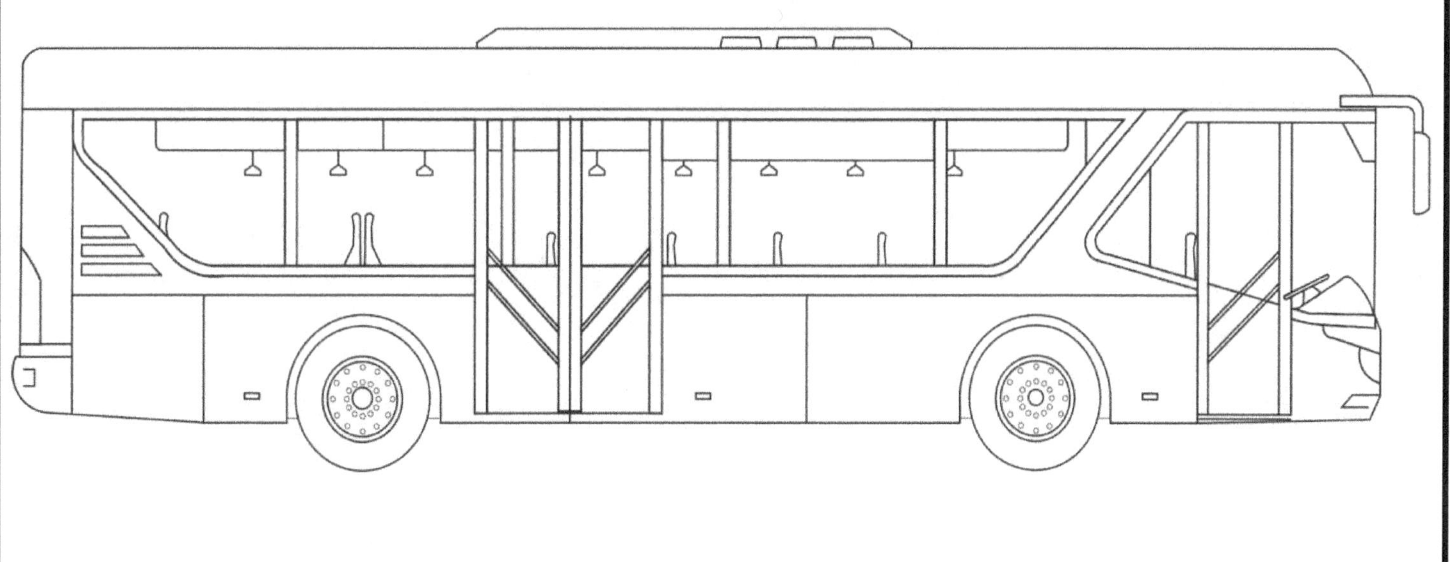

BICYCLE - BICICLETA

CAR – AUTO

SUBMARINE – SUBMARINO

HELICOPTER - HELICOPTERO

TRAIN – TREN

GRASS CUTTER – CORTADORA DE HIERBA

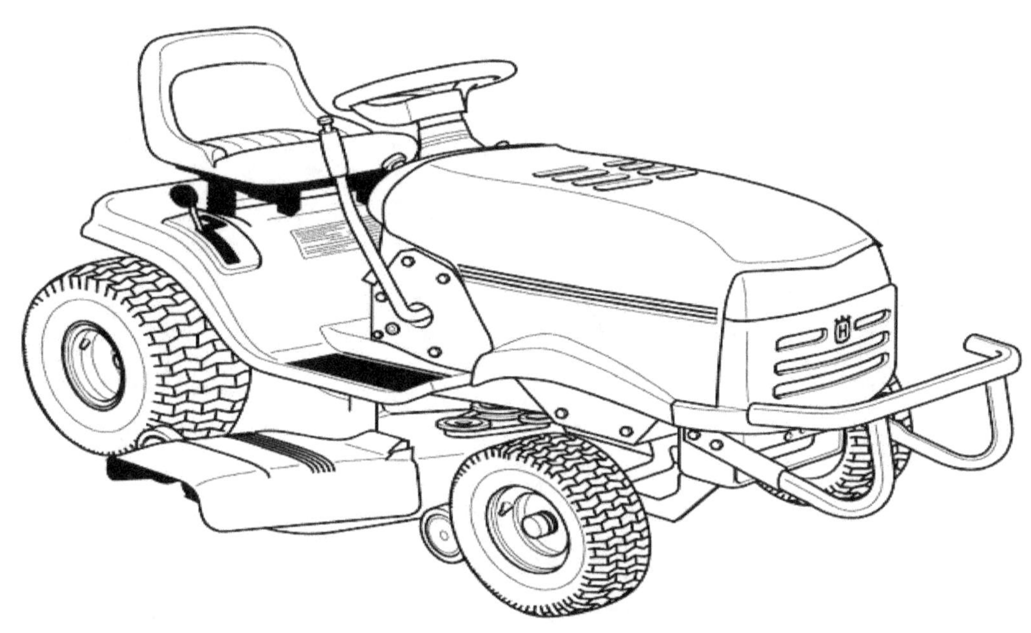

TRUCK – CAMION

MOTORCYCLE – MOTOCICLETA

VAN – CAMIONETA

EXCAVATOR – EXCAVADORA

MOTOR GRADER – MOTONIVELADORA

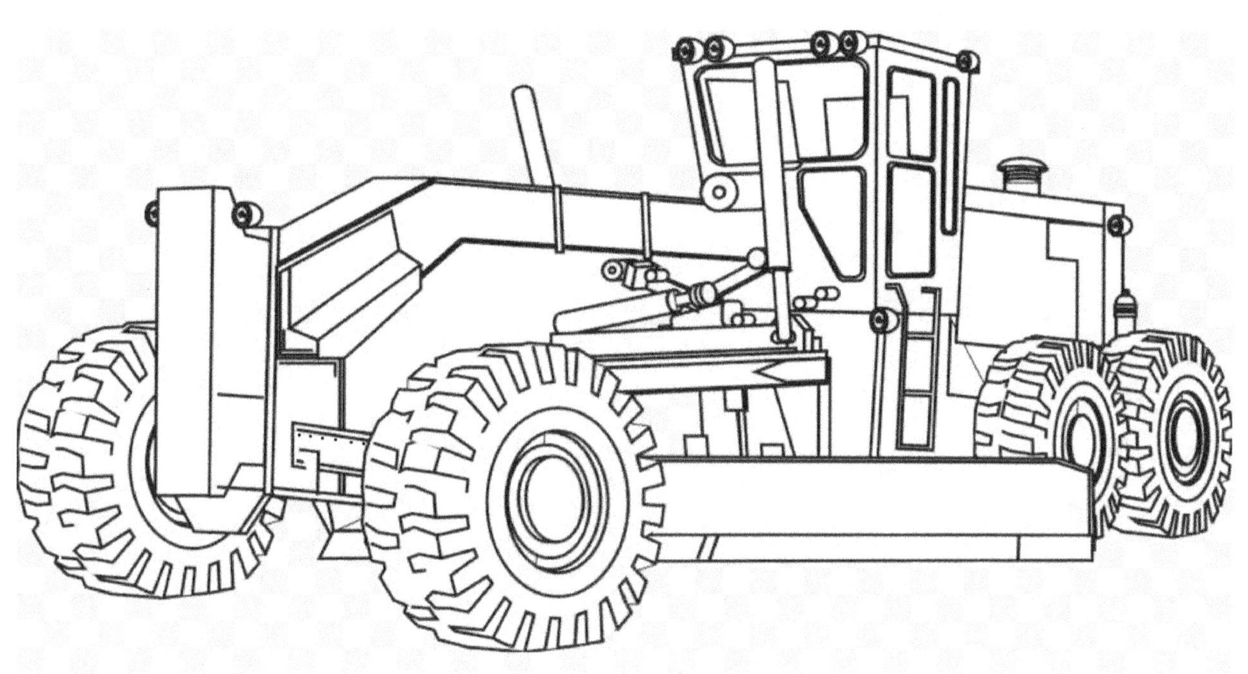